JACKET POTATO REQUIRED

75 MOUTHWATERING RECIPES FOR THE BAKED POTATO

BY IAN MANSELL

© IAN MANSELL 2010

CONTENTS

1)   Introduction

Long live the humble potato!

The variety of ways to cook, serve, and even drink (hic) make the humble spud one of the most versatile foods of all time.

There are also many ways to cook them be it fried, chipped, boiled, steamed, mashed and of course baked. The baked potato is surely of the healthiest meals to enjoy but it is also one of the most underrated of meals lacking in the amount of good ideas and recipes attached to it.

In this book we will show you what recipes there are on offer, ranging from the simple but gorgeous baked beans through to the lavish filet mignon.

Variety of Potato.

Most large potatoes will suffice but there are a variety of potatoes available locally that can make your baked spud meal that little bit more special. The ideal potatoes include: King Edwards, Maris Piper, Desiree, Estima, and Cara, but there are many others on offer and are certainly worth a try and especially look out for some locally grown potatoes ask about those from your local potato merchant or greengrocer. But the ultimate of course is to grow your own.

2)   Nutritional Values

I love eating jacket potatoes because I enjoy them, but course the nutritional value has to be taken into account, indeed gone are the days that dieting consisted of cardboard, cardboard, with a dash of cardboard.

These days medical advice say that we should have an intake of more unrefined starchy foods including of course the humble potato also including rice and pasta. We all know that fried or chipped potatoes are not the answer to a healthy balanced diet but baked, steamed, and boiled certainly are.

The case for the jacket potato

To those who enjoy their meals with potatoes should look again at the baked spud as I will prove with the recipes contained within this book that everybody can enjoy a good meal or snack with some of the world's best recipes and ingredients.

So with great pleasure I commend the following recipes to your oven. Enjoy!

3) The Perfect Jacket Potato?

I cannot and will not preach to you about the 'perfect' baked potato, but instead I will give you some guidelines of approaching a good spud but of course the final judgement will depend on which equipment you will utilise, either the oven or microwave.

To oven cook the potatoes:

1) Pre heat the oven to 210c / gas mark 7
2) Wash the potatoes thoroughly and then prick them all over with a fork and then spray or brush them with olive oil or butter as desired.
3) When the oven has reached temperature reduce the heat to 200c / gas mark 6.
4) Finally place them on a baking tray lined with foil and place them in the oven for up to one hour (dependent on size of potato) or until the flesh has softened.

To microwave the potatoes:

Scrub and then prick the potatoes with a fork then place them in the microwave with kitchen roll on the base. Brushing with oil or butter is not recommended.

Set the microwave on high and the general rule of thumb is 5-6 minutes per potato* or 17-20 minutes for four potatoes* or again until the flesh has softened.

*Based on 750 watt microwave.

The timings for the following recipes are for the fillings only and don't include timings for the potatoes.

4) Recipes: Quick, Simple, but Nice

There are many simple and tasty dishes to enjoy including:

Baked Beans, Cheese, or even Cottage Cheese with its various flavours and of course not forgetting Tuna, Chicken, or Prawn Mayonnaise.

So the following dishes although simple to prepare are also very tasty.

Cheddar Cheese and Crispy Bacon

Cooking Time 15 Minutes - Serves 2

2 Baking Potatoes

100g/4oz Rindless Back Bacon Diced

2tbsp Olive Oil

1 medium sized onion finely chopped

25g/1oz butter

50g/2oz fine Cheddar cheese grated (strength to suit taste)

1. Cook your jacket potato (for cooking instructions see chapter 3)
2. Mix the finely chopped onion and diced bacon together
3. Heat the olive oil in a frying pan and empty the bacon and onion into the pan and gently fry for up to 5 minutes or until the onion is soft and golden.
4. Drain off the excess liquid and then cook again at higher temperature until both bacon and the onion are both crispy.
5. Slice the cooked potatoes in half and then scoop out the potato flesh into a bowl then add the butter and mash the potato and then season to taste (do not discard the skins)
6. Place the bacon and onion along with half of the grated cheese and mix into the mashed potato and then fill the potato skins
7. Place the remaining cheese over the potatoes and then grill until melted

BLT Brunch Time

Cooking Time 20 Minutes - Serves 4

4 Baking Potatoes

8 Rindless Back Bacon rashers

2tbsps Olive Oil

6 Spring onions finely sliced

400g can chopped tomatoes

2 garlic cloves crushed

8 crispy Iceberg lettuce leaves

3tbsps mayonnaise

Pinch of paprika (optional)

1. Cook your jacket potato (for cooking instructions see chapter 3)
2. Heat the oil in a pan and cook the spring onions and garlic until softened
3. Stir in the chopped tomatoes and then bring to the boil and then simmer for around 7 minutes
4. Grill the bacon until it has become crisp
5. Slice the cooked potatoes in half
6. Place the lettuce leaves on the potato halves and then place the tomatoes and top it off with the bacon and the mayonnaise and as an added option try a pinch of paprika for that little extra bite

Smoked Salmon with Scrambled Eggs

Cooking Time 6 Minutes - Serves 4

4 Baking Potatoes

4 eggs

50g/2oz butter

Pinch of nutmeg

Pinch of cayenne pepper

5tbsps milk

100g/4oz smoked salmon cut into strips

Salt and pepper for seasoning

1. Cook your jacket potato (for cooking instructions see chapter 3)
2. Place your eggs in a bowl along with the milk, seasoning, cayenne and nutmeg and beat with a whisk until frothy
3. Slice the cooked potatoes in half and scrape the surface with a fork to form a little mash and for the eggs to sit
4. Melt the remaining butter in a pan and then pour in the egg mixture, cook the mixture over a low heat and stir constantly to achieve your scrambled egg
5. When the scrambled egg is almost set add your salmon to the pan for around 30 seconds and then place on your potatoes
6. Season for taste

Sausages with Beans & Cheese

Cooking Time 15 Minutes - Serves 4

4 Baking Potatoes

4 Thick Pork Sausages

400g Can of Baked Beans

100g/4oz Good Cheddar Cheese grated

25g/1oz Butter

5tbsps milk

Few shakes of Worcester sauce

1. Cook your jacket potato (for cooking instructions see chapter 3)
2. Grill your sausages for around 12 – 14 minutes or until cooked through, then cut each sausage into bite size pieces
3. When the potatoes are nearly cooked through, gently heat the baked beans in a saucepan and when hot add your sausages, grated cheese and a few shakes of Worcester sauce for that extra bite
4. Slice a lid of your potatoes and place them aside. Scoop out the flesh of the potato and place in a bowl. Mash the potato and then add the butter and milk for a final whisk and then place the mash back into the skins
5. Finally spoon your mixture of beans, sausage and cheese onto your potatoes and serve

Yorkshire Ham & Wensleydale Cheese

Cooking Time 12 Minutes - Serves 2

2 Baking Potatoes

2 Good slices of Yorkshire ham (sliced into strips)

75g/3oz Wensleydale or Wensleydale Blue Cheese (grated or crumbled)

25g/1oz Butter

1tsp horseradish sauce or Yorkshire sauce (if available)

5tbsps crème fraiche

1. Cook your jacket potato (for cooking instructions see chapter 3)
2. Grate or crumble your cheese
3. With the potatoes cooked slice in half and scoop out the flesh, then mash well and then add the butter and do a final whisk
4. Place some of the cheese aside and then add the rest into the potato along with the horseradish sauce and the Yorkshire ham and whisk well
5. Replace the potato back into the potato skins and then return them to the oven to heat through for around 12 minutes
6. Place on dish and top with the crème fraiche and the remainder of the cheese

Marmite, Mayonnaise & Spring Onion

Cooking Time 1 Minute - Serves 1

1 Baking Potatoes

2tsp Marmite

2tbsps mayonnaise

1 spring onion (finely sliced)

1. Cook your jacket potato (for cooking instructions see chapter 3)
2. Put a cross cut into your potato and press on the 4 quarters to create a bloom
3. Place your mayonnaise into a small bowl and then add the marmite and mix well
4. When complete, mix in the spring onion and then place mixture onto the potato

5) Recipes: Meat

Chilli con Carne

Cooking Time 30 Minutes - Serves 4

4 Baking Potatoes

500g lean steak mince

1 finely chopped onion

2tbsps sunflower oil

2 garlic cloves (crushed)

400g can of chopped tomatoes

400g can of red kidney beans

0.5 – 1 tsp chilli powder (some like it hot)

1tsp ground cumin

1tsp oregano

0.5 tsp Tabasco sauce (optional)

Salt (seasoning)

1. Cook your jacket potato (for cooking instructions see chapter 3)
2. Heat the oil in a wok or saucepan and fry the onion until soft and golden. Then add the steak mince and cook until brown. Drain off any excess liquid.
3. Add the garlic, chilli powder, cumin, oregano, and Tabasco sauce (if required) and stir.
4. Then add the chopped tomatoes, kidney beans and season.
5. Simmer for 25 minutes.
6. Cross cut the potatoes and push down the four quarters and then top with the mixture.

Spicy Spanish Chorizo with Tomato

cooking Time 30 Minutes - Serves 4

4 Baking Potatoes

125g/5oz chorizo (sliced)

1 finely chopped large onion

2tbsps olive oil

2 garlic cloves (crushed)

400g can of chopped tomatoes

1tsp paprika

0.5 chilli powder (optional)

1. Cook your jacket potato (for cooking instructions see chapter 3)
2. Heat the oil in a pan or wok and fry the onions until soft and light brown then add the paprika and garlic for a further 2 minutes
3. Stir in the chopped tomatoes and slowly bring to the boil, then add the chorizo to the pan and reduce the heat and simmer for 20-25 minutes
4. Cross cut the cooked potatoes and push down the 4 quarters for the potato bloom. Finally add the mixture to the potatoes and serve.

Hungarian Pork Goulash

Cooking Time 15 Minutes - Serves 4

4 Baking Potatoes

454g/1lb boneless pork chops (sliced)

1 finely chopped medium onion

1tbsp olive oil

25g/1 oz butter

1 garlic clove (crushed)

125ml/4fl oz white wine

2tsps paprika

250ml/8fl oz soured cream

1tbsp Dijon mustard

Salt and pepper (to season)

1. Cook your jacket potato (for cooking instructions see chapter 3)
2. Heat the oil and the butter in a pan or wok and stir-fry the pork is browned and cooked through, then season and set aside.
3. Add the paprika and onion to the pan and cook until the onion is soft. Stir in the white wine, sour cream, and mustard then whisk until fully blended and smooth heat up but do not boil.
4. Return the pork to the pan and heat through.
5. Finally cross cut the cooked potatoes and gently press the 4 quarters down and then add the mixture and garnish (optional) with paprika.

Italian Special

Cooking Time 15 Minutes - Serves 4

4 Baking Potatoes

454g/1lb lean steak mince

1 finely chopped medium onion

2tbsp olive oil

2 garlic cloves (crushed)

200g/8oz sliced mushrooms

250g/10oz spinach (sliced)

Pinch of nutmeg

Pinch of oregano

100g/4oz parmesan cheese

Salt and pepper (to season)

1. Cook your jacket potato (for cooking instructions see chapter 3)
2. Heat oil in a pan or wok on medium to high heat
3. Place the onion and garlic and cook until tender and then add the mushrooms and cook until tender.
4. Place the spinach in pan and warm through and then a pinch of oregano and nutmeg along with seasoning to taste.
5. Cross slice your potatoes and then carefully press the potato downwards for the flower look then add the mixture and to finish sprinkle the parmesan cheese over.

Mexican Pork

Cooking Time 15 Minutes - Serves 4

4 Baking Potatoes

4 Boneless pork loin chops

1tsp chilli powder

1tsp ground cumin

0.5tsp cayenne pepper

1 garlic clove crushed

0.5tsp salt

2tbsps olive oil

1 green bell pepper (sliced)

1 medium onion (sliced)

4oz soured cream

4oz salsa

1 avocado (diced)

1tbsp chopped fresh coriander

1 lime cut into wedges

1. Cut the loin chops into thin strips and set aside and then combine the chilli powder, cumin, cayenne, salt and garlic into a coating or plastic bag and shake well to mix the ingredients together and then add the pork chop strips and shake well to enable a good coating to the meat. Place in the fridge overnight or at the least four or five hours.
2. Cook your jacket potato (for cooking instructions see chapter 3)
3. Heat the olive oil in your pan or wok to a high setting
4. Add the green pepper and cook until tender then place the onion in and fry until tender then remove and set aside.
5. Change to medium setting and add the coated pork and cook until tender and is fully cooked and then return the onions and pepper to the pan to heat through.
6. Cross slice your potatoes and press to achieve the flower look and then add the mixture evenly.
7. To finish top the mixture with the salsa and cream along with the avocado and coriander.
8. Serve the meal with the lime wedges for that finishing touch.

Monday's Pot Luck

Cooking Time 20 Minutes - Serves 4

4 Baking Potatoes

1tsp olive oil

12oz sliced meat leftovers

400g canned chopped tomatoes

3 red chilli's or suit to taste (finely diced)

0.5tsp chilli powder

1 onion (sliced)

6oz cheddar cheese (grated) or cheese of your choice

1. Cook your jacket potato (for cooking instructions see chapter 3)
2. Heat the olive oil in your pan or wok to a medium setting then add your onion and chilli's and cook until the onions are golden.
3. Then add the meat, tomatoes, chilli powder and bring to the boil and then add your 5oz of cheese and bring the heat to a simmer and let the cheese melt into the mixture.
4. Cross slice your potatoes and press to achieve the flower look and then add the mixture evenly.
5. To finish top the mixture with the remaining cheese and serve.
6. This is a pot luck meal so you can add any ingredient as you like.

Beef with Ale

Cooking Time 30 Minutes - Serves 4

4 Baking Potatoes

2tbsps olive oil

500g beef pieces

4oz plain flour

1 medium onion (diced)

100g/4oz mature cheddar cheese (grated)

400ml real ale beer or stout

0.5 tsp English mustard powder

Salt & pepper seasoning to taste

1. Cook your jacket potato (for cooking instructions see chapter 3)
2. Heat the olive oil in your pan or wok to a medium setting then add your onion until golden.
3. Dice the beef pieces and coat them in flour and the mustard and season to taste and then place in the pan and cook until tender.
4. Slowly stir in the ale and bring it to the boil and then simmer for five minutes.
5. Cut your potatoes in half and then scoop out the flesh and mash with 75g/3oz of the cheese and then mix the mash in with the beef mixture and return to the potatoes.
6. To finish sprinkle the remaining cheese over the potatoes.

Turkish Delight

Cooking Time 15 Minutes - Serves 4

4 Baking Potatoes

2tbsps olive oil

300g lean beef mince

300g lamb mince

1 medium onion (finely diced)

2 garlic cloves (crushed)

100ml/4oz passata

1tsp dried oregano

1tsp cinnamon

0.5tsp ground cumin

1tsp salt

0.5tsp freshly ground black pepper

1 green bell pepper deseeded and finely chopped

6 cherry tomatoes finely sliced

1. Cook your jacket potato (for cooking instructions see chapter 3).
2. Heat the olive oil in your pan or wok to a high setting then add your onion, meats and garlic until cooked and the meats are brown.
3. Drain off all the excess fat from the pan and add the passata, herbs and spices bring to the boil and then simmer over a low heat for five minutes.
4. Cross cut the potatoes and press for the flower effect and then place the ready mixture over them and garnish with the green peppers and the cherry tomatoes.

Jambalaya (simple version)

Cooking Time 40 Minutes - Serves 4

4 Baking Potatoes

400g chopped tomatoes

275g/10oz easy cook rice

1 red pepper (de-seeded and finely chopped)

1 large chorizo sausage (sliced)

600ml/1pt hot chicken stock

110g/4oz frozen sweetcorn

½ tsp Cajun seasoning or more to taste

1. Cook your jacket potato (for cooking instructions see chapter 3).
2. Tip the rice into a pan or wok along with the other ingredients and then add the hot chicken stock and then cook over a medium high heat until the rice has fluffed out.
3. The mixture might require further water until the rice is fully cooked.
4. Cross slice the potatoes and press for the flower effect and add the mixture.

Greek Pork Raita

Cooking Time 30 Minutes - Serves 4

4 Baking Potatoes

4 lean boneless pork chops

60ml/2floz olive oil

60ml/2floz lemon juice

2tbsp Dijon mustard

2 garlic cloves (crushed)

1tsp dried oregano

0.5tsp dried thyme

1tbsp olive oil (for cooking)

1 tomato (de-seeded and diced for garnishing)

1. Slice the chops into strips and place in a mixing or plastic bag and then place the olive oil, lemon juice, mustard, garlic and the herbs into a bowl and mix well. Place the mixture over the pork and mix well. Place the pork in your fridge for at least 6 hours or overnight.
2. Cook your jacket potato (for cooking instructions see chapter 3).
3. Remove the pork and drain and the marinade can now be discarded.
4. Heat a wok or pan over a medium heat and add the olive oil for cooking to the pan and then add the pork until the meat has been cooked completely.
5. Cross slice the potatoes and press down for flower effect and then place the pork on to the potatoes.

TO MAKE THE CUCUMBER AND MINT RAITA SAUCE

250ml/8fl oz natural yoghurt

½ Cucumber (finely chopped)

Handful of mint leaves (finely chopped) or dried mint

Pinch of salt

1. Wrap the cucumber in kitchen towel and squeeze the excess water out.
2. Mix all the ingredients together and chill in the fridge
3. Serve over the pork and finish off with tomato garnish

Worcester Brown

Cooking Time 25 Minutes - Serves 4

4 Baking Potatoes

8 slices Rindless back bacon (cut to small pieces)

2tbsps olive oil

1 small onion (finely chopped)

3tbsps plain flour

300ml/10floz milk

1 ½ tsp Worcester sauce

½ tsp dried English mustard

1tbsp sherry

100g/4oz mature cheddar (grated)

225g/8oz cooked chicken (diced)

100g/4oz parmesan cheese

1. Cook your jacket potato (for cooking instructions see chapter 3).
2. Heat your wok or pan over a medium heat and add the olive oil and then add the onion and cook until golden and add the bacon pieces. When cooked whisk in the flour and cook until thickened then add the milk and continue to whisk until the texture is bubbly.
3. Add the Worcester sauce, mustard and sherry and stir in. Add the cheese while stirring continuously finally add the cooked chicken to warm through.
4. Cross slice the potatoes and press down for flower effect and then place the mixture on to the potatoes.
5. Sprinkle the parmesan cheese over the top and finally place until a grill for the final bubbly effect.

Liver with Orange Pate

Cooking Time 20 Minutes - Serves 4

4 Baking Potatoes

175g/6oz smooth liver pate

60g/2oz cream cheese

2tbsps natural yoghurt

Salt & pepper (for seasoning)

Grated zest of ½ orange

2tbsps orange juice

1. Cook your jacket potato (for cooking instructions see chapter 3).
2. Place the pate, cream cheese and yoghurt and whisk until mixed and slightly softened.
3. Slice the potatoes in half and remove the flesh and mash the flesh until soft and fluffy and then mix the mixture into the mash and then stir in the orange zest and juice.
4. Place the mixture back into the skins and return to the oven for up to 15 minutes to heat through.

Sausage with Butter Beans

Cooking Time 30 Minutes - Serves 4

4 Baking Potatoes

12 pork chipolatas (cut into 4 pieces)

1tbsp olive oil

1 onion (finely diced)

1 celery stick (finely chopped)

2 garlic cloves (crushed)

75ml/2 ½ fl oz white wine

400g can of chopped tomatoes

3tbsps tomato puree

1tsp paprika

400g butter beans

Salt & pepper (to season)

1tbsp chopped parsley (to garnish)

1. Cook your jacket potato (for cooking instructions see chapter 3).
2. Heat the pan or wok on a medium high heat and place oil in the pan followed by the chipolatas until browned and completely cooked. Remove and rest.
3. Retain the juices in the pan and add the onion, celery, and garlic and cook until soft then turn the heat to high and add the wine and let it bubble for a few moments then add the canned tomatoes and tomato puree with the paprika and seasoning then bring to the boil. Reduce the heat and simmer for around 20 minutes or until thickened.
4. Add the cooked sausages and the drained butter beans and simmer for a further 10 minutes.
5. Cross slice the potatoes and press for the flower effect and add the mixture. Finally add the parsley garnish.

Sweet & Sour Pork

Cooking Time 45 Minutes - Serves 4

4 Baking Potatoes

340g/12oz lean pork (diced)

2tbsps cornflour

4tbsps sunflower oil

1 onion (finely sliced)

1tbsp tomato puree

1 garlic clove (crushed)

1tbsp dark soy sauce

2tbsps white wine vinegar

2tbsps clear honey

1tbsp sherry

280ml/ ½ pint chicken stock

2.5cm/1inch piece root ginger (grated)

½ green pepper (de-seeded and sliced)

½ red pepper (de-seeded and sliced)

1. Cook your jacket potato (for cooking instructions see chapter 3).
2. Toss the diced pork into the cornflour.
3. Heat the pan or wok on a medium high heat and place halve the oil in the pan followed by the onions and fry until cooked. Remove and rest.
4. Add the remaining oil and fry the pork until browned and completely cooked through and then return the onion to the pan.
5. Add the remaining ingredients and bring to the boil then reduce the heat and simmer for around 30 minutes or the meat is tender
6. Cross slice the potatoes and press for the flower effect and add the mixture.

Creamy Bacon with Mushrooms

Cooking Time 10 Minutes - Serves 4

4 Baking Potatoes

6 rashers Rindless unsmoked back bacon (diced)

60g/2oz butter

2 garlic cloves (crushed)

6 spring onions (finely sliced)

225g/8oz chestnut mushrooms (sliced)

1tsp cornflour

Small amount of milk

Pinch grated nutmeg

200g/7oz fromage frais

Salt & pepper to taste

1. Cook your jacket potato (for cooking instructions see chapter 3).
2. Melt the butter in a pan or wok and cook the bacon and garlic until browned then stir in the chopped spring onions and mushrooms for up to 5 minutes or the mushrooms are soft.
3. Mix the cornflour to a paste with the small amount of milk and then stir into the pan. Add the grated nutmeg then stir in the fromage frais and bring the cream slowly up to simmering point and let it simmer for two minutes and then season.
4. Cross slice the potatoes and press for the flower effect and add the mixture.

6) Recipes: Chicken

Chicken & Mushroom Curry

Cooking Time 30 Minutes plus 2 hours standing time - Serves 4

4 Baking Potatoes

4 Chicken Breasts (boneless) cut into bite size pieces

½ tsp chilli powder

1 ½ tsp garam masala

2.5cm/1inch peeled and grated root ginger

2 cloves crushed garlic

3tbsps olive oil

1tbsp medium curry paste (or hot if desired)

1 medium onion finely chopped

400g chopped tomatoes

200g finely chopped chestnut mushrooms

Seasoning to taste

1. Cook your jacket potato (for cooking instructions see chapter 3)
2. Place your chicken in a bowl and add the chilli powder, garam masala, ginger and garlic and stir in to coat the chicken well. Allow the chicken to absorb the flavours for around 2 hours.
3. Heat 2tbsps of the olive oil in a wok or pan and add the flavoured chicken and curry paste and then cook over a high heat for around five minutes or until the chicken has browned. Once this has been achieved remove from the pan and set aside.
4. Add the remaining oil to the pan and fry the onion until golden soft for around 5 minutes and then return the chicken to the pan then add the mushrooms and cook for 2 minutes.
5. Finally add the tomatoes to the pan and bring to the boil and then simmer for around 10 minutes. Cut the potatoes in half and then top off with the curry and serve.

Thai Style Chicken Breast

Cooking Time 20 Minutes - Serves 4

4 Baking Potatoes

4 Chicken Breasts (boneless) cut into bite size pieces

1 onion (finely sliced)

2tbsps sunflower oil

1tbsp Thai green curry paste (milder version use Thai red)

200ml/7floz can coconut milk

1tsp light soy sauce

½ lime (zest and juice)

1tbsp fresh coriander (finely chopped)

1tbsp sugar

1. Cook your jacket potato (for cooking instructions see chapter 3)
2. Heat the oil in a wok or pan on a high heat and the fry the onion and chicken for around 5 minutes or until the onion has softened and the chickens is fully cooked then stir in the garlic and cook for a further 2 minutes and then remove from the pan and set aside.
3. Add the curry paste and cook for a minute then add half of the milk to the pan and stir, boil on a high heat for 2-3 minutes. Return the chicken to the pan and then stir in the lime zest, juice, soy sauce and sugar and then simmer gently for a further 5 minutes.
4. Finally stir in the remaining coconut milk and simmer until heated through. Cut your cooked potatoes in half and then top off with the chicken.

Chicken and Cream Cheese Melt

Cooking Time 15 Minutes - Serves 4

4 Baking Potatoes

1oz butter

1 large onion (finely sliced)

2 chicken breasts (boneless and cubed)

225g/8oz cream cheese

2 diced and de-seeded green chilli's

120ml/4floz milk

2 spring onions (finely chopped)

Salt & pepper to taste

50g/2oz mature cheddar cheese (grated)

Dash of Worcester sauce (optional)

1. Cook your jacket potato (for cooking instructions see chapter 3)
2. Heat the butter in a wok or pan and fry the onions for around 5 minutes or until soft and golden. Add the chicken and cook for 2 minutes and then add the cream cheese and stir gently until the cream cheese begins to melt.
3. Add the chilli and the spring onions and thin the mixture a little with milk then season to taste. Cross cut the potatoes and gently push down on the four quarters to obtain the flower effect and then divide the mixture evenly over the potatoes and finish off with the grated cheese on top and the optional dash of Worcester sauce.

Chicken Romana

Cooking Time 15 Minutes - Serves 4

4 Baking Potatoes

2 chicken breasts (boneless and cubed)

3tbsp olive oil

1 garlic clove (crushed)

150g/5oz button mushrooms (sliced)

1 onion (diced)

1 jar artichoke hearts (drained and coarsely chopped)

240ml/8floz passata sauce

50g/2oz grated parmesan cheese

1. Cook your jacket potato (for cooking instructions see chapter 3)
2. Pour 2tbsp olive into wok or pan and fry the chicken on a medium heat until completely cooked through then remove and set aside.
3. Add the remaining oil to the pan and fry the garlic and onion for around 5 minutes until golden and soft then add the mushrooms until cooked through.
4. Add the artichoke hearts and then stir in the passata sauce and heat through.
5. Cross cut the potatoes and then press gently to obtain the flower effect and then divide the mixture evenly and finish off with a sprinkling of parmesan cheese.

Chicken of the Orient

Cooking Time 15 Minutes - Serves 4

4 Baking Potatoes

2 chicken breasts (boneless and cubed)

2tbsp olive oil

1 onion (diced)

2 carrots (finely chopped)

2 celery stalks (finely chopped)

1 jar Teriyaki Sauce

1. Cook your jacket potato (for cooking instructions see chapter 3)
2. Add 1tbsp of the oil into a wok or pan and add the diced chicken until cooked through, remove and set aside.
3. Add the remaining oil to the pan and fry the onion until soft then add the carrots and celery and cook until tender. Return the chicken to the pan and then add the teriyaki sauce mix thoroughly and heat through.
4. Cross cut the potatoes and gently push down to achieve the flower effect and then divide the mixture evenly over the potatoes.

Grecian Style Chicken

Cooking Time 40 Minutes - Serves 4

4 Baking Potatoes

2tbsps olive oil

1 onion (finely sliced)

1 garlic clove (crushed)

1 carrot (finely diced)

350g/12oz cooked shredded chicken (or turkey)

180ml/6floz passata sauce

120ml/4floz red wine

¼ tsp ground allspice

¼ tsp red chilli flakes

½tsp ground black pepper

1tsp ground cinnamon

1 bay leaf

1. Cook your jacket potato (for cooking instructions see chapter 3)
2. Add the oil to a wok or pan and cook the onion on a medium high heat until soft then add the garlic and the carrot and cook for 3 minutes.
3. Add the remaining ingredients and then simmer for 30 minutes stirring occasionally and then remove the bay leaf.
4. Finally cut the potatoes in half and divide the mixture over the top.

Smoked Chicken and Tarragon Mousse

Cooking Time 5 Minutes - Serves 4

4 Baking Potatoes

225g/4oz smoked chicken breast

1 lemon (zest and Juice)

1tbsp chopped tarragon

3tbsps mayonnaise

2tbsps Dijon mustard

Salt & pepper to taste

1. Cook your jacket potato (for cooking instructions see chapter 3)
2. Cut the chicken into small pieces and place in a food processor and then add the rest of the ingredients and then blitz the mixture until it is coarsely chopped.
3. Cross cut the potatoes and gently press down for the flower effect and then divide the mixture evenly.

Coronation Chicken

Cooking Time 5 Minutes - Serves 4

4 Baking Potatoes

350g/12oz cooked chicken

1tbsp olive oil

1 shallot (finely chopped)

1tsp curry paste (mild or hot) according to taste

1tbsp tomato puree

Dash of Worcester sauce

110g/4oz mayonnaise

6 apricot halves (canned in fruit juice drained)

1. Cook your jacket potato (for cooking instructions see chapter 3)
2. Heat the oil in a wok or pan and cook the shallot until softened and then add the curry paste and cook over a low heat for 1 minute then add the tomato puree and Worcester sauce. Remove from the heat and set aside to cool.
3. Put the mixture in a food processor along with the mayonnaise and apricots and blitz until the mixture becomes a smooth paste.
4. Cut the chicken into small pieces and place in a bowl and then add the rest of the mixture and stir in.
5. Cross cut the potatoes and gently press down for the flower effect and then divide the mixture evenly.

Chicken al la King

Cooking Time 20 Minutes - Serves 4

4 Baking Potatoes

500g/1lb 2oz cooked chicken (chopped)

2tbsp sunflower oil

60g/2oz butter

1 onion (finely sliced)

1 red pepper (de-seeded and finely chopped)

1 green pepper (de-seeded and finely chopped)

175g/6oz button mushrooms (sliced)

25g/1oz plain flour

1tsp paprika

200ml/7floz milk

250ml/8floz chicken stock

Salt & pepper to taste

1. Cook your jacket potato (for cooking instructions see chapter 3)
2. Place the oil and the butter in a wok or pan and fry the onion until softened and then add the peppers and cook for 5 minutes. Stir in the mushrooms and cook for 5 minutes.
3. Mix in the flour and paprika with salt and pepper for seasoning and remove the pan from the heat. Pour in the chicken stock and mix in well and then gently stir in the milk.
4. Return the pan to a simmering heat and continue to stir until the sauce has come to the boil and thickened.
5. Gradually stir in the chicken and mix well and then leave on simmer for a further 5 minutes until the chicken has heated through.
6. Cross cut the potatoes and gently press down for the flower effect and then divide the mixture evenly.

Chicken Jalfrezi

Cooking Time 30 Minutes - Serves 4

4 Baking Potatoes

2tbsps sunflower oil

2tsp ground cumin

2tsp yellow mustard seeds

1tsp ground turmeric

2tbsps masala curry paste

2.5cm/1in fresh root ginger (peeled and finely grated)

3 garlic cloves (crushed)

1 onion (finely sliced)

1 red pepper (de-seeded and sliced)

½ green pepper (de-seeded and sliced)

2 chicken breasts (boned and diced)

225g can chopped tomatoes

3tbsps chopped coriander

1. Cook your jacket potato (for cooking instructions see chapter 3)
2. Heat the oil in a wok or large pan then add the cumin, mustard seeds, turmeric and curry paste and fry while stirring for 2 minutes. Add the ginger, garlic, and onion and fry until the onion softens then add the peppers and the chillies and continue to fry for 5 minutes.
3. Further increase the heat and then add the chicken and fry until almost brown then add the tomatoes and coriander then simmer for 10 minutes or the chicken is completely cooked through.
4. Cross cut the potatoes and gently press down for the flower effect and then divide the mixture evenly.

Coq au Vin

Cooking Time 1hr 30 Minutes - Serves 4

4 Baking Potatoes

2tbsps plain flour

Salt & pepper to season

4 chicken breasts (boned and diced)

50g/2oz butter

125g/4½ oz pancetta (cut to thick short strips)

2 garlic cloves (crushed)

1 carrot (cubed)

1 celery stick (roughly chopped)

4tbsps brandy

750ml/1 ½ pints red wine

1 bay leaf

4 sprigs of thyme

1tbsp olive oil

450g/1lb button onions

1tsp brown sugar

1tsp red wine vinegar

225g/8oz button mushrooms

1. Cook your jacket potato (for cooking instructions see chapter 3)
2. Season the flour with the salt and pepper seasoning to taste and coat the chicken with approx 1tbsp of the flour then melt half the butter in a wok or large pan and add the chicken and cook until the chicken is golden brown all over.
3. Add the pancetta, garlic, carrot, and celery then fry until softened stir in the remaining flour and cook for 2 minutes. Pour in the brandy and wine and stir to remove any sediment that may form add the bay leaf and thyme bring to the boil and then simmer for 1 hour.
4. Mix in the onions and mushrooms to the chicken and cook for a further 20 minutes
5. Remove the chicken and vegetables from the pan and boil the sauce for 5 minutes until reduced and return to the chicken.
6. Cross cut the potatoes and gently press down for the flower effect and then divide the mixture evenly.

Tarragon Chicken al la Crème

Cooking Time35 Minutes - Serves 4

4 Baking Potatoes

4 chicken breasts (boned and diced)

25g/1oz butter

1tbsp rapeseed oil

250g/9oz shallots (sliced)

1tsp dried herbes de Provence

2 garlic cloves (finely chopped)

250ml/8floz hot chicken stock

120ml/4floz dry white wine

250g/9oz crème fraiche

2tbsps chopped tarragon

1. Cook your jacket potato (for cooking instructions see chapter 3)
2. melt the butter with the oil in a wok or pan, add the chicken and fry for 3 minutes or until golden brown then turn them over and repeat for a further 2 minutes.
3. Add the shallots, dried herbs, garlic, and salt and pepper to taste then add the stock and wine and bring to the boil. Reduce the heat to low and then simmer for 25 minutes.
4. Lift out the chicken and bring the stock back to the boil until the sauce has reduced by around half. Stir in the crème fraiche and the chopped tarragon and continue cooking until thickened. Finally place the cooked chicken back into the sauce.
5. Cross cut the potatoes and gently press down for the flower effect and then divide the mixture evenly.

Pot Chicken

Cooking Time20 Minutes - Serves 4

4 Baking Potatoes

350g/12oz cooked chicken (boned and diced)

2 carrots (diced)

2 parsnips (peeled and diced)

600ml/1pint hot chicken stock

25g/1oz butter

1 onion (finely chopped)

2 celery stalks (finely chopped)

20g/ ¾ oz plain flour

½ tsp mustard powder

250ml/8floz double cream

Salt & pepper to season

1. Cook your jacket potato (for cooking instructions see chapter 3)
2. Place the carrots and parsnips in a pan along with the stock and boil over a high heat for around 5 minutes or the vegetables are tender.
3. Meanwhile in another pan or wok melt the butter over a medium heat and add the onion and celery and cook stirring frequently for around 5 minutes or until tender. Add the flour and continue stirring for 2 minutes. Stir in the stock gradually and then bring to the boil then reduce the heat and simmer for 2 minutes.
4. Stir in the peas, mustard and the salt and pepper to taste and add the root vegetables and cook for a further 2 minutes or until warmed through.
5. Cross cut the potatoes and gently press down for the flower effect and then divide the mixture evenly.

Chicken Mayonnaise with a Difference

Cooking Time 10 Minutes - Serves 4

4 Baking Potatoes

350g/12oz cooked chicken (boned and shredded)

3tbsps Mayonnaise

2tsp chopped tarragon

1 ½ tsp wholegrain mustard

1tsp lemon juice

Salt & pepper to season

1. Cook your jacket potato (for cooking instructions see chapter 3)
2. Mix together all the ingredients except the chicken and stir until you have a good mixture and then season with the salt and pepper and then add the chicken and stir well.
3. Cross cut the potatoes and gently press down for the flower effect and then divide the mixture evenly.

Crunchy Chicken and Sweetcorn Topping

Cooking Time 5 Minutes - Serves 4

4 Baking Potatoes

350g/12oz cooked chicken (boned and shredded)

2 celery sticks (finely sliced)

1 300g tin sweetcorn (drained and washed)

150ml crème fraiche

Salt and pepper to taste

1tbsp chopped fresh mint

Dash of Tabasco sauce

1. Cook your jacket potato (for cooking instructions see chapter 3)
2. Place the chicken, celery and sweetcorn in a bowl then add the crème fraiche, seasoning, mint, and Tabasco sauce into the mixture and stir until coated.
3. Cross cut the potatoes and gently press down for the flower effect and then divide the mixture evenly.

7) Recipes: Vegetarian.

Bubble & Squeak

Cooking Time 20 Minutes - Serves 4

4 Baking Potatoes

25g/1oz butter

1 onion (finely diced)

340g/12oz cooked cabbage

100g/4oz cooked carrots

50g/2oz cooked Swede

Salt & pepper to taste

1. Cook your jacket potato (for cooking instructions see chapter 3)
2. Melt the butter in a wok or pan and cook the onion over a low heat until soft. Add the rest of the ingredients into the pan for a further 3-4 minutes or until heated through.
3. Cut the potatoes in half and scoop the flesh out into a bowl and mash until fluffy. Place the mash into the pan and stir well until the mixture is well combined and then season to taste. Cook for a further 10 minutes or until warmed through and finally scoop the mixture back into the skins and serve.

Vegetable Curry

Cooking Time 45 Minutes - Serves 4

4 Baking Potatoes

2tbsps sunflower oil

1 onion (diced)

2 garlic cloves (crushed)

2tsps ground coriander

1tsp ground cumin

½ tsp ground fenugreek

½ tsp ground turmeric

½ tsp chilli powder

175g/6oz cauliflower florets (cut small)

2 carrots (diced)

1 red pepper (de-seeded and diced)

1 green pepper (de-seeded and diced)

120g/4oz button mushrooms (halved)

120g/4oz green beans (cut short lengths)

4tbsps natural yoghurt

3tbsps crème fraiche

1tsp cornflour (optional)

1. Cook your jacket potato (for cooking instructions see chapter 3)
2. Heat the oil in a wok or large pan and cook the onion on a medium heat for around 5 minutes or until soft then reduce to low heat and add the garlic and the spices to the pan and stir constantly for around 3 minutes to prevent burning.
3. Place the vegetables in and stir over the heat for around 4 minutes then add the stock and bring to the boil. Reduce the heat and then simmer for 30 minutes or until the vegetables are tender. *If required you can thicken the liquid by adding the cornflour to a little water and mix until it is a paste and then add to the liquid*.
4. Finally stir in the yoghurt and the crème fraiche and heat gently.
5. Cut the potatoes in half and then spoon over the mixture and serve.

Baked Bean Special

Cooking Time 35 Minutes - Serves 4

4 Baking Potatoes

2tbsps sunflower oil

1 onion (diced)

2 garlic cloves (crushed)

400g/14oz can chopped tomatoes

1tsp dried mixed herbs

1tbsp wholegrain mustard

2 x 432g/15 ½ oz haricot or cannellini beans (drained and rinsed)

Salt & pepper to taste

1. Cook your jacket potato (for cooking instructions see chapter 3)
2. Add the oil to the wok or pan and cook the onion and garlic for 4 minutes or until soft.
3. Pour the chopped tomatoes, herbs, and the beans into the pan then bring to the boil and then simmer on a low heat for 25 minutes or the beans are tender and then season to taste.
4. Cut the potatoes in half and then spoon over the mixture and serve.

Potato Soufflé with Carrot & Asparagus

Cooking Time 40 Minutes - Serves 2

2 Baking Potatoes

175g/6oz carrots (finely sliced)

½ onion (diced)

15g/ ½ oz butter

2tsps plain flour

6tbsps milk

2 eggs (separated)

Salt & pepper to taste

Grated nutmeg (pinch)

½ bunch asparagus

½ orange

1. Cook your jacket potato (for cooking instructions see chapter 3)
2. Bring a small pan of water to the boil and add the carrots and the onion, then cook for 10 minutes or until tender. Drain the water and place in a food processor.
3. Melt the butter in the pan and stir in the flour and cook over a very low heat for 1 minute then remove from the heat and gradually add the milk and stir well after each addition.
4. Return the pan to the heat and continue to cook over a very low heat stirring constantly until thickened. Pour the mixture over the carrots and process the mixture until smooth.
5. Beat in the egg yolks, season with salt, pepper and the nutmeg then place the carrot mixture into a bowl. When the potatoes are done, cut in half and scoop the flesh out and mash well and then mix it into the carrot mixture.
6. Whisk the egg whites until peaks form and then carefully fold them into the mixture and then pile back into the skins and return to the oven for 15-20 minutes or until risen and golden.
7. Meanwhile, cook the asparagus in boiling water for 6-8 minutes until just tender and grate the zest off the orange and squeeze the juice.
8. Finally serve the asparagus with the finished potatoes and sprinkle a little orange juice over the asparagus with a little zest and nutmeg.

Turkish Vegetable Supreme

Cooking Time 60 Minutes - Serves 4

4 Baking Potatoes

3tbsps olive oil

2 onions (diced)

2 garlic cloves (crushed)

1tbsp ground coriander

1tbsp ground cumin

1tsp ground turmeric

½ tsp ground cardamom

2x400g chopped tomatoes

85g/3oz sultanas

2tbsp chopped coriander

1tbsp chopped mint

1tbsp chopped parsley

1. Cook your jacket potato (for cooking instructions see chapter 3)
2. Heat the oil in a wok or large pan and fry the onion and garlic over a medium heat for 4 minutes or until softened and then add the spices and cook until you achieve a fragrant smell and then stir in the tomatoes and bring to the boil and then reduce the heat to simmer for 30 minutes or the mixture has reduced.
3. Add the sultanas, chopped coriander, mint and parsley and heat for 4 minutes. Meanwhile slice the cooked potatoes in half and scoop the flesh out into a bowl and mash until fluffy and then add it to the mixture.
4. Finally scoop the mixture back into the skins and return them to the oven for 20 minutes and then serve.

Carrot & Parsnip Puree with Tarragon

Cooking Time 15 Minutes - Serves 4

4 Baking Potatoes

5 carrots (peeled and chopped)

2 parsnips (peeled and chopped)

1tbsp olive oil

100ml/3 ½ fl oz double cream

2tsp chopped tarragon

Salt & pepper to taste

1. Cook your jacket potato (for cooking instructions see chapter 3)
2. Bring a pan of lightly salted water to the boil and cook the carrots for 5 minutes on a high heat and then add the parsnips and bring to the boil and then reduce to simmer for a further 5 minutes or the vegetables are tender.
3. Drain and shake off any excess water and place in a food processor and blend to a paste, while the processor is still running add the cream.
4. Cut the cooked potatoes in half and scoop the flesh into a bowl and mash until fluffy. Blend the mash and the puree together and scoop the mixture back into a saucepan and place on a very low heat until warmed through and finally scoop the mixture back into the skins and serve.

Spud within a Spud

Cooking Time 55 Minutes - Serves 4

4 Baking Potatoes

4 sweet potatoes

4tbsps olive oil

150ml/5fl oz double cream (a little extra for drizzling)

1tbsp horseradish cream

Salt & pepper to taste

1. Cook your jacket potato (for cooking instructions see chapter 3)
2. Also cook the sweet potatoes with the same instructions and when cooked peel the sweet potato skins off and discard.
3. Place the cooked flesh into a food processor, season to taste and process to a puree and while the processor is still running add the oil and the cream to the mix.
4. Cross slice the baked potatoes and gently push down to create the flower effect and place the puree on top. Finally add some horseradish cream (optional) on top along with a little cream and serve.

The Italian Job

Cooking Time 20 Minutes - Serves 4

4 Baking Potatoes

400g artichoke hearts (drained and chopped)

1 garlic clove (crushed)

3 plum tomatoes (coarsely chopped)

225g/8oz mixed olives (stoned and sliced)

2tbsps olive oil

1tbsp chopped parsley

1tsp Italian seasoning

150g/5oz parmesan cheese (grated)

Salt & pepper to taste

1. Cook your jacket potato (for cooking instructions see chapter 3)
2. Heat the oil in a wok or pan and fry the onion and garlic over a medium high heat for 4 minutes or until soft. Add the artichokes, tomatoes, olives, and heat through.
3. Add the herbs to the pan and mix through. Cross slice the potato and gently push down for the flower effect and top it with the mixture.
4. Finally sprinkle over the grated cheese and serve.

Sauté Vegetable with Pesto

Cooking Time 15 Minutes - Serves 4

4 Baking Potatoes

2tbsps olive oil

1 garlic clove (crushed)

2 carrots (finely sliced)

2 celery sticks (finely sliced)

1 onion (diced)

1 red pepper (de-seeded and sliced)

1 courgette (finely sliced)

225g/8oz button mushrooms (halved)

190g/7oz jar green pesto

150g/5oz parmesan cheese (grated)

Salt & pepper to taste

1. Cook your jacket potato (for cooking instructions see chapter 3)
2. Heat the oil in a wok or pan and fry the onion, garlic, carrots, celery, and cook on a medium high heat for 5 minutes or until soft. Then add the pepper, courgette, and mushrooms and cook until beginning to brown off, then stir in the pesto and warm through.
3. Cross slice the potato and gently push down for the flower effect and top it with the mixture.
4. Finally sprinkle over the grated cheese and serve.

Mexican Delight

Cooking Time 20 Minutes - Serves 4

4 Baking Potatoes

2tbsps olive oil

3 garlic clove (crushed)

1 onion (diced)

1 green chilli (chopped)

400g/14oz can red kidney beans (drained and washed)

400g/14oz can pinto beans (drained and washed)

2tbsps chopped coriander

150ml/ 5floz vegetable stock

25g/1oz cheddar cheese (grated)

Salt & pepper to taste

RELISH:

4 spring onions (finely sliced)

1 red onion (finely sliced)

1 green chilli (chopped)

1tbsp garlic wine vinegar

1tsp caster sugar

1 tomato (diced)

1. Cook your jacket potato (for cooking instructions see chapter 3)
2. Heat the oil in a wok or pan and fry the onion over a medium heat for 4 minutes and then add the garlic and chilli and cook for a further minute.
3. Mash the beans and then stir into the pan along with the coriander, and then stir in the stock and cook the beans for around 5 minutes or until soft and pulpy. Stir frequently to prevent catching on the base of the pan.
4. Mix the relish ingredients together in a bowl.
5. Cross slice the potato and gently push down for the flower effect and top it with the mixture. Finally sprinkle the grated cheese over the top and serve with the relish.
6. Finally sprinkle over the grated cheese and serve.

8) Recipes: Fish & Seafood.

Scampi in Vino Pesto

Cooking Time 25 Minutes - Serves 4

4 Baking potatoes

50g/2oz butter

2 garlic cloves (crushed)

450g/1lb fresh scampi

3tbsps white wine

1 jar red pesto

1 small jar passata

50g/2oz fresh parsley (finely chopped)

1. Cook your jacket potato (for cooking instructions see chapter 3)
2. Heat the butter in a wok or pan and add the garlic and cook over a medium high heat until soft then add the scampi and stir fry until almost opaque. Then add the wine, pesto, and passata to heat through.
3. Cross slice the cooked potatoes and gently press down to create the flower effect and then serve the mixture on top.

Salmon with Creamed Dill Sauce

Cooking Time 15 Minutes - Serves 4

4 Baking Potatoes

25g/1oz butter

340g/12oz salmon fillets

4tbsps dry white wine

1tbsp chopped fresh dill

6tbsps crème fraiche

Salt & pepper to taste

1. Cook your jacket potato (for cooking instructions see chapter 3)
2. Melt the butter in a wok or pan and cook the salmon for 3-4 minutes on each side and then remove from the pan and flake the salmon and discard the bones and skin.
3. Pour the wine into the pan and bring to the boil for 1 minute then add the dill and stir in the crème fraiche and boil for around 3 minutes or until slightly thickened. Finally add the salmon to the mixture and warm through.
4. Cross slice the baked potatoes and gently push down to create the flower effect and place the mixture on top and serve.

Tuna with Tricolour Peppers

Cooking Time 15 Minutes + Reheating Time 10 Minutes - Serves 4

4 Baking Potatoes

2tbsps olive oil

½ green pepper (de-seeded and diced)

½ red pepper (de-seeded and diced)

½ yellow pepper (de-seeded and diced)

½ tsp dried chillies

2.5cm/1inch piece root ginger (peeled and grated)

200g/7oz tuna chunks (drained)

Grated zest of ½ lemon

1tbsp lemon juice

60g/2oz cheddar cheese (grated)

Salt & pepper to taste

1. Cook your jacket potato (for cooking instructions see chapter 3)
2. Heat the oil in a wok or pan and place the peppers in over a medium heat for around the 5 minutes until soft stir often to prevent burning then add the ginger and chillies and season with salt and pepper.
3. Add the tuna, lemon zest, and juice into the pan and cook over a low heat for around 3 minutes making sure the tuna is hot.
4. Once the potatoes are cooked, slice them in half and scoop out the flesh and place into a bowl. Mash well. Add the tuna mixture to the mash and mix well.
5. Scoop the mixture back into the skins and sprinkle over the top with grated cheese and return the potatoes to the oven for approx 10 minutes or until the cheese has melted. Then serve.

Smoked Haddock with Tomato

Cooking Time 20 Minutes - Serves 4

4 Baking Potatoes

225g/8oz smoked haddock (skinned and boned)

4tbsps milk

25g/1oz butter

Pinch of grated nutmeg

1 beef tomato (chopped)

1 tsp chopped fresh parsley

Salt & pepper to taste

1. Cook your jacket potato (for cooking instructions see chapter 3)
2. Place the fish in an ovenproof dish and pour in the milk and add the butter then season with salt and pepper. Cover the dish with foil.
3. With 20 minutes to go before the potatoes are cooked place the fish on the lower shelf in the oven and cook it until the fish can easily be flaked.
4. Cut a lid off the cooked potatoes and discard then scoop out the flesh from the skins and place in a bowl. Add the liquid from the fish and the nutmeg then season to taste, then mash well.
5. Pile the tomato pieces and the parsley into the bowl and mix well with the mash and then replace the flesh back into the skins. Finally place the flaked fish on top of the mash and serve.

Prawn with Avocado

Cooking Time 2 Minutes - Serves 4

4 Baking Potatoes

1 ripe avocado (peeled and cubed)

½ lime (grated zest and Juice)

120g/4oz prawns (cooked and peeled)

1 tomato (skinned and chopped)

4tbsps Greek yoghurt

1tbsp tomato puree

Dash of Tabasco

Salt & pepper to taste

Ground paprika

1. Cook your jacket potato (for cooking instructions see chapter 3)
2. Place the avocado pieces into the lime juice to stop discolouration and add the prawns and tomato, stir in well.
3. Put together yoghurt, tomato puree, Tabasco, seasoning and lime zest into a bowl then add to the prawns then stir to ensure a good coating.
4. Cross slice the potatoes and gently press down to create the flower effect then top it off with the prawns and a sprinkling of paprika and serve.

Kipper & Egg Mash

Cooking Time 30 Minutes - Serves 2

2 Baking Potatoes

225g/8oz undyed smoked kippers

1 hard-boiled egg (roughly chopped)

2tbsps frozen peas (defrosted)

1tbsp red Leicester cheese (grated)

1tbsp Cheddar cheese (grated)

Salt & pepper to taste

1. Cook your jacket potato (for cooking instructions see chapter 3)
2. Cook the kippers as per the pack instructions and then place the chopped egg into a bowl followed by the peas and the fish after flaking the flesh.
3. With the potatoes cooked, cut in half and scoop out the flesh and mash well and then add to the fish. Stir the fish and the mash together and season to taste.
4. Scoop the mixture back into the skins. Combine the two cheeses together and then sprinkle on top and then return to the oven for around 15 minutes to heat through and melt the cheese.

Sea Bass Creole

Cooking Time 25 Minutes - Serves 4

4 Baking Potatoes

2tbsps sunflower oil

1 onion (diced)

1 garlic clove (crushed)

1 red chilli (de-seeded and chopped)

½ green pepper (de-seeded and chopped)

400g/14oz can chopped tomatoes

1 bay leaf

½ tsp mixed herbs

340g/12oz sea bass fillets (cubed)

175g/6oz prawns (cooked and peeled)

25g/1oz butter

Salt & pepper to taste

Dash of Tabasco

1. Cook your jacket potato (for cooking instructions see chapter 3)
2. Heat the oil and fry the garlic and onion for around 4 minutes or until soft, then add the chilli and green pepper and cook for a further 3 minutes. Put in the herbs, bay leaf and tomatoes and simmer for 5 minutes.
3. Add the fish and cook gently for around 12 minutes and then add the prawns and continue for a further 5 minutes.
4. With the potatoes cooked do a deep cross slice and remove the flesh and place into a bowl. Add the butter, seasoning, and a dash of Tabasco and mash well. Return the mash back into the skins and then finally remove the bay leaf and spoon the mixture on top.

Crab & Prawn Delight

Cooking Time 20 Minutes - Serves 2

2 Baking Potatoes

170g/5 ½ oz crab meat (tinned)

60g/2oz prawns (cooked and peeled)

4 spring onions (finely sliced)

60ml/4tbsps mayonnaise

½ lime (zest and juice)

Salt & pepper to taste

1. Cook your jacket potato (for cooking instructions see chapter 3)
2. Place the crab meat in a bowl along with the prawns and the spring onions.
3. Combine the mayonnaise, lime zest and juice and stir. Add the mixture to the crab and stir well.
4. When cooked, slice the potatoes in half and scoop out the flesh and mash well. Stir in the crab mixture and combine well and then season to taste.
5. Finally scoop the mixture back into the skins and return to the oven for around 12 minutes to heat through.

Crab Mornay

Cooking Time 20 Minutes - Serves 4

4 Baking Potatoes

50g/2oz butter

50g/2oz parsley (finely chopped & diced)

4 spring onions (finely sliced)

1tbsp plain flour

175g/6oz single cream

100g/4oz gruyere cheese

1tbsp sherry

350g/12oz fresh crab meat

Salt & pepper to taste

1. Cook your jacket potato (for cooking instructions see chapter 3)
2. Melt the butter in a wok or pan and place the onions and parsley over a medium heat for around 4 minutes or until soft then sprinkle in the flour and stir in to combine.
3. Stir in the cream and stir until the mixture is smooth and then slowly add the cheese and continuously stir until the cheese has melted. Then add the sherry and then season to taste.
4. Add the crab to the mixture and heat through.
5. Cross slice the potatoes and gently push down for the flower effect and then add the mixture.

Smoked Salmon Brunch

Cooking Time 10 Minutes - Serves 4

4 Baking Potatoes

200g/8oz salmon (finely sliced)

50g/2oz butter

4 spring onions (finely sliced)

100g/4oz gruyere cheese (grated)

4 eggs (scrambled) *optional*

Salt & pepper to taste

1. Cook your jacket potato (for cooking instructions see chapter 3)
2. Melt the butter in a wok or pan and place the onions over a medium heat for around 4 minutes or until soft. Add the salmon to the pan to warm through.
3. Cross slice the potatoes and gently push down for the flower effect and then add the mixture. Finally place the scrambled egg over the top (optional) and finish off with some grated cheese.

Prawns with Parmesan Cream Potato

Cooking Time 15 Minutes - Serves 4

4 Baking Potatoes

16 Raw king prawns (peeled and deveined)

2tbsps olive oil

155g/4oz pancetta (diced)

4 spring onions (finely sliced)

2 garlic cloves (crushed)

4tbsps crème fraiche

1 lemon (juice)

Salt & pepper to taste

50g/2oz parmesan cheese (grated)

1. Cook your jacket potato (for cooking instructions see chapter 3)
2. Melt the oil in a wok or pan and place the pancetta over a medium heat for around 5 minutes. Add the spring onions, garlic and cook for a further 3 minutes.
3. Add the prawns and cook until they turn pink but do not overcook them. Then add the crème fraiche and bring to the boil. Pour in the lemon juice and then season to taste. Reduce the heat to simmer for around 2 minutes
4. Slice the cooked potatoes in half and scoop out the flesh and mash well, then add the prawn mixture and combine well. Scoop the flesh back into the skins.
5. Finally finish off with some grated parmesan cheese.

Hot & Sour Prawns

Cooking Time 15 Minutes + Marinade Time 4 hours - Serves 4

4 Baking Potatoes

2tbsps soy sauce (dark)

1tbsp sunflower oil

2tbsps rice wine vinegar

1tsp sugar

1-2 crushed red chilli flakes (according to taste)

2 garlic cloves (crushed)

300g/12oz medium sized prawns (peeled and uncooked)

4 spring onions (sliced)

200g/8oz mushrooms (sliced)

100g/4oz snow peas (trimmed and sliced finely)

1. Mix together soy sauce, vinegar, sugar, red chilli flakes, garlic, and the sesame oil. Add the prawns and marinade for 4 hours or overnight.
2. Cook your jacket potato (for cooking instructions see chapter 3)
3. Melt the oil in a wok or pan and place the onions over a medium heat for around 2 minutes or until soft then add the mushrooms and cook for a further 2 minutes then add the snow peas and cook for 1 minute.
4. Add the prawns and marinade into the pan and stir fry until the prawns are pink
5. Slice the cooked potatoes in half and scoop out the flesh and mash well, then add the prawn mixture and combine well. Scoop the flesh back into the skins.

Ensaladilla Rusa – Russian Salad

Cooking Time 25 Minutes - Serves 4

4 Baking potatoes

Salt & pepper for taste

1 carrot (finely diced)

115g/4oz frozen peas

90ml/3floz mayonnaise

2 roasted red peppers (drained and sliced into small strips)

200g can tuna (drained)

2 hard boiled eggs (coarsely chopped)

1. Cook your jacket potato (for cooking instructions see chapter 3)
2. Cook the diced carrot in a saucepan for around 6 minutes almost tender then add the peas and cook for a further 3 minutes.
3. Slice the cooked potatoes in half and scoop out the flesh, place in a bowl and mash well, then add the mayonnaise, carrots and peas and the eggs and combine well. Finally add the tuna and mix well then scoop the flesh back into the skins and serve.

Crab Mayonnaise with a Difference

Cooking Time 0 Minutes - Serves 4 No Cooking

4 Baking potatoes

Salt & pepper for taste

4tbsps mayonnaise

1.5cm/ ½ inch piece of ginger (peeled and grated)

227g/8oz white crabmeat

1tbsp coriander leaves (chopped)

2 spring onions (finely sliced)

1 red chilli (deseeded and finely chopped) *for garnish*

1 lime (grated zest and juice)

1. Cook your jacket potato (for cooking instructions see chapter 3)
2. Mix together the crabmeat, ginger, lime zest and juice, mayonnaise, coriander and spring onions and then season to taste.
3. Cross slice the cooked potatoes and press gently to create the flower effect and then place the mixture on top. Finally sprinkle the red chillies on top to garnish.

Baked Supreme

Cooking Time 25 Minutes - Serves 4

4 Baking potatoes

Salt & pepper for taste

200g can white crabmeat

2 spring onions (finely sliced)

40g/1 ½ oz butter

1tbsp sunflower oil

1 carrot (peeled and diced)

2 celery stalks (trimmed and finely chopped)

50g/2oz Cheddar cheese (grated)

1. Cook your jacket potato (for cooking instructions see chapter 3)
2. Heat the oil in a wok or pan and cook the carrot and celery for 2 minute on a medium high heat and then continue to cook on a medium heat for around 5 minutes or are tender.
3. Slice the cooked potato in half and scoop out the flesh into a bowl then add the butter and mash well. Add the cooked vegetables into the mash then follow on with the spring onions and the crabmeat then fold in well. Season to taste.
4. Finally scoop the mixture back into the skins and sprinkle the cheese over the top and then return the potatoes back to the oven for a further 12 minutes or until the cheese is bubbling.

9) Recipes: Dairy, Cheese & Eggs.

Coleslaw with Smoked Austrian Cheese

Cooking Time 5 Minutes - Serves 4

4 Baking potatoes

½ small head of white cabbage (finely shredded)

2 carrots (grated)

½ green pepper (de-seeded and finely sliced)

90g/3oz Austrian smoked cheese (cubed)

4tbsps mayonnaise

4tbsps sour cream

Salt & pepper to taste

1. Cook your jacket potato (for cooking instructions see chapter 3)
2. Place the cabbage in a bowl along with the carrot and green pepper and cheese. Combine the mayonnaise and the cream then season well, add the mixture to the cabbage and stir until everything is coated.
3. Slice the cooked potatoes in half and serve the coleslaw on top.

Blue Stilton with Walnut Dressing

Cooking Time 5 Minutes - Serves 4

4 Baking potatoes

1 apple (sliced)

Lemon juice

4 celery stalks (sliced)

60g/2oz walnuts (chopped)

150g/5oz Greek yoghurt

60g/2oz blue Stilton cheese (crumbled)

Salt & pepper to taste

1. Cook your jacket potato (for cooking instructions see chapter 3)
2. Toss the sliced apple into some lemon juice to prevent it discolouring.
3. Add the celery, apple, and walnuts into a bowl and add the yoghurt. Crumble in the cheese and mix all the ingredients together until everything is coated.
4. Cross-slice the cooked potatoes and gently press down to achieve the flower effect. Spoon the mixture on top, season and serve.

Glamorgan Tatties

Cooking Time 15 Minutes - Serves 4

4 Baking potatoes

60g/2oz butter

454g/1lb leeks (thinly sliced)

25g/1oz plain flour

280ml/ ½ pint milk

90g/3oz local mature cheese (grated)

Salt & pepper to taste

1. Cook your jacket potato (for cooking instructions see chapter 3)
2. Melt the butter in a wok or pan and cook the leeks over a low heat for up to 10 minutes or until they are soft and then stir in the flour and cook for 1 minute.
3. Remove the pan from the heat and gradually add the milk while continuing to stir well. Return the pan to the heat and continue to cook over a low heat and stir constantly until thickened. Add the cheese to the sauce and gently stir in the cheese until it melts.
4. Slice the cooked potatoes in half and scoop out the flesh and mash well. Add the leek mixture to the mash and stir until fully combined. Return the mixture to the skins and serve.

Somerset Brie Melts

Cooking Time 15 Minutes - Serves 4

4 Baking potatoes

225g/8oz Somerset Brie

225g/8oz cottage cheese

8 spring onions (sliced)

Salt & pepper to taste

Pinch of grated nutmeg

1. Cook your jacket potato (for cooking instructions see chapter 3)
2. Remove any rind from the brie and discard. Mash the brie and the cottage cheese together until both cheeses are fully mixed then add the spring onions and season with salt, pepper, and a little grated nutmeg.
3. Slice the top of the cooked potatoes and set the lid aside then scoop out the flesh and mash well. Beat the mash into the cheese mixture and return it to the skins. Reposition the lids and return the potatoes to the oven for up to 15 minutes or until the cheese melts then serve.

Cheesy Herb Potato

Cooking Time 10 Minutes - Serves 2

2 Baking potatoes

1 onion (finely chopped)

25g/1oz butter

1tbsp fresh rosemary (chopped)

1tbsp fresh thyme (chopped)

1tbsp fresh sage (chopped)

2tbsps cream cheese

25g/1oz red Leicester cheese (grated)

25g/1oz local mature cheese (grated)

Salt & pepper to taste

Parsley (chopped) to garnish

1. Cook your jacket potato (for cooking instructions see chapter 3)
2. Melt the butter in a wok or pan and cook the onions for around 4 minutes or until soft then add the rosemary, thyme, sage, and then season and combine.
3. Slice the cooked potatoes in half and remove the flesh from the skins and then mash well and then add the cream cheese and mix well. Add the potato mixture to the pan and combine and cook until hot.
4. Place the mixture back into the skins and fluff up with a fork. Sprinkle the red Leicester cheese on two halves and the local mature cheese on the other two halves and then return to the oven until the cheese has melted. Remove from oven, garnish with parsley and serve.

Eggs Florentine in a Jacket

Cooking Time 25 Minutes - Serves 2

2 Baking potatoes

90g/3oz frozen spinach (chopped)

25g/1oz butter

2 eggs

1tbsp cornflour

120ml/4floz milk

2tbsps Parmesan cheese (grated)

Salt & pepper to taste

Pinch of grated nutmeg

1. Cook your jacket potato (for cooking instructions see chapter 3)
2. Place the spinach in a small pan and over a low heat cook until it starts to defrost, then add the butter and cook for around 3 minutes and season with salt, pepper and nutmeg.
3. Poach the eggs in simmering water until the eggs are just set, then remove and place in cold water until required.
4. Empty the cornflour into a pan and add a little milk to form a smooth paste then over a low heat stir in the remaining milk and stir until the sauce thickens, season then pour in half of the Parmesan cheese and stir until melted.
5. Slice the tops off the cooked potatoes and scoop out the flesh and then mash well. Once down repack the mash into the skins and leave a hollow at the top.
6. Spoon the spinach mixture into the two potatoes and then remove the eggs from the cold water and drain well, once dried place on top of the spinach.
7. Finally spoon over the remaining sauce and sprinkle the remaining cheese and return to the oven for 15 minutes. Remove and serve.

Greek Salad

Prep Time 15 Minutes - Serves 4

4 Baking potatoes

400g/14oz plum tomatoes (small chunks)

½ cucumber (peeled, de-seeded, chunks)

150g/5 oz feta cheese (drained and small cubes)

100g/3 ½ oz black olives (pitted and sliced)

½ lemon (juice)

Fresh basil (handful, finely chopped)

2tbsps extra virgin olive oil

Salt & pepper to taste

1. Cook your jacket potato (for cooking instructions see chapter 3)
2. Place the tomatoes, cucumber, feta, olives and basil into a bowl and place in the fridge until needed.
3. Cross-slice the cooked potatoes and gently press them down for the flower effect and then add the salad and drizzle the olive oil over and season to taste and finally drizzle a little lemon juice and serve.

Indian Potato and Egg Jackets

Cooking Time 12 Minutes - Serves 4

4 Baking potatoes

4 eggs (hard-boiled and coarsely chopped)

3 celery sticks (finely chopped)

2 spring onions (finely chopped)

1 green pepper (de-seeded and finely chopped)

1-2tsps curry paste (mild or hot according to taste)

2tbsps single cream

3tbsps mayonnaise

2tsps mango chutney

Paprika to taste

1. Cook your jacket potato (for cooking instructions see chapter 3)
2. Place the chopped egg, celery, spring onions, and green pepper into a bowl.
3. Mix together in another bowl, the curry paste, cream, mayonnaise and chutney and stir until combined then pour the mixture over the chopped eggs and stir well.
4. Slice a lid off the cooked potatoes and scoop out the flesh and mash well then add the mash to the egg mixture and mix well, then return the mixture back to the skins.
5. Return the potatoes to the oven for 10 minutes to heat through. Remove and serve.

Three Cheese Topping with Mayonnaise

Cooking Time 8 Minutes - Serves 4

4 Baking potatoes

110g/4oz mature Cheddar cheese (grated)

110g/4oz red Leicester cheese (grated)

50g/2oz Gruyere cheese (grated)

3tbsps mayonnaise

1 spring onion (finely diced) to garnish

1. Cook your jacket potato (for cooking instructions see chapter 3)
2. Slice a lid off the cooked potatoes and scoop out the flesh and mash well then add all the cheese and mayonnaise and mix well, and then return the mixture back to the skins.
3. Return the potatoes to the oven for 10 minutes to heat through. Remove then garnish with the spring onions and serve.

Welsh Rarebit

Cooking Time 8 Minutes - Serves 4

4 Baking potatoes

25g/1oz butter

225g/8oz strong local cheese (grated)

1tbsp English mustard powder

3tbsps real or brown ale

Worcester sauce (to taste)

1. Cook your jacket potato (for cooking instructions see chapter 3)
2. Cross-slice the cooked potatoes and gently press them down for the flower effect.
3. Melt the butter in a wok or pan over a low heat then add the cheese, mustard powder and the ale and cook until creamy and slightly bubbly then stir the sauce over the potatoes and drizzle Worcester sauce over the top, according to taste and then return to the oven to heat through for around 4 minutes. Remove and serve.

10) Recipes: Special Delights

Steak al la Crème

Cooking Time 10 Minutes - Serves 4

4 Baking potatoes

25g/1oz butter

275g/10oz lean fillet steak (sliced into thin strips)

150ml/5floz sour cream

1tbsp horseradish

2tsp Dijon mustard

1tsp salt

200g/7oz cheddar cheese (grated)

2 spring onions (finely sliced)

1. Cook your jacket potato (for cooking instructions see chapter 3)
2. Mix the horseradish, mustard, sour cream, and salt in a bowl and set aside.
3. Melt the butter in a wok or pan and add the steak and cook over a high heat until the steak is done to your liking e.g. for rare 1-2 minutes. Remove the steak from the pan and set aside.
4. Finally cross slice the cooked potatoes and gently push down for the flower effect then place the cream mixture on top followed by the steak then a sprinkling of cheese and then top with the spring onions.

Smoked Salmon with Caviar

Cooking Time 25 Minutes - Serves 4

2 Baking potatoes

90g/3oz smoked salmon pate

2tbsps crème fraiche

Salt & pepper to taste

1tbsp lemon juice

2tsps fresh dill (chopped)

2 small sprigs fresh dill

2tsps lumpfish caviar

1. Cook your jacket potato (for cooking instructions see chapter 3)
2. Slice the cooked potato in half and scoop the potato out into a bowl and mash well.
3. Beat the pate in a bowl until the pate has softened a little then mix in the crème fraiche until combined.
4. Mix the pate mixture into the potato and then season to taste. Add the lemon juice and the dill and stir.
5. Finally return the mixture back to the skins and return to the oven for around 12 minutes or until heated through. Then serve topped with the caviar and sprigs of dill to garnish.

Posh Nosh

Cooking Time 25 Minutes - Serves 4

4 Baking potatoes

75g/3oz butter

275g/10oz lean fillet steak (sliced into thin strips)

1 onion (diced)

50g/2oz shitake mushrooms (sliced)

50g/2oz button mushrooms (sliced)

½ tsp dried thyme

150ml/5floz sour cream

Salt & pepper to taste

1. Cook your jacket potato (for cooking instructions see chapter 3)
2. Melt 1oz of the butter in a wok or pan and add the steak and cook over a high heat until the steak is done to your liking e.g. for rare 1-2 minutes. Remove the steak from the pan and set aside.
3. Add the remaining butter to the pan and fry the onions for around 4 minutes or until soft, then add the mushrooms and cook until tender and season to taste.
4. Return the meat to the pan along with the herbs and the sour cream and heat through.
5. Finally cross slice the cooked potatoes and gently push down for the flower effect then place the mixture on top.

Salmon Rillettes

Cooking Time 5 Minutes - Serves 4

4 Baking potatoes

50g/2oz butter

250g/9oz hot smoked salmon (skinned)

4tbsps Greek yoghurt

½ lemon (finely grated zest & juice)

2tbsps fresh chives (snipped)

50g jar salmon caviar

50g/2oz fresh watercress (finely chopped) to garnish

Lemon wedges to garnish

1. Cook your jacket potato (for cooking instructions see chapter 3)
2. Place the butter in a bowl and beat it until smooth, then flake the salmon into small pieces and mash it with the butter. Add the yoghurt, lemon zest, juice and the chives and fold into the mixture.
3. Cross slice the cooked potatoes and gently press down to create the flower effect and then serve the mixture on top followed by a helping of caviar and then garnish with the watercress and lemon wedges.

Top Toff Nosh

Cooking Time 15 Minutes - Serves 4

4 Baking potatoes

50g/2oz butter

2 baby leeks (finely sliced)

200g/7oz chestnut mushrooms (sliced)

1tsp tarragon

2tbsps plain flour

1tbsp white wine

240ml/8floz chicken stock

200g/7oz Brie (cubed and rind removed)

Salt & pepper to taste

1. Cook your jacket potato (for cooking instructions see chapter 3)
2. Melt the butter in a wok or pan and add the leeks over a medium high heat and cook until tender and then the mushrooms and cook until tender.
3. Stir in the tarragon and the flour and then add the wine and stock and then bring to a gentle boil.
4. Stir in the cheese until fully melted and season to taste.
5. Cross slice the potatoes and gently press down to get the flower effect and place the mixture on top and serve.

11) Further Information

For more information and more recipes or even if you have a recipe yourself.

Go to: www.jacketpotatorequired.co.uk